Rob Feldman's

CARTOONS, COMICS, and COWS in CARS

LITTLE-KNOWN FACTS ABOUT THE AUTHOR

Did YOU know that:

Rob Feldman is NOT an elite gymnast.

However, he wants you to know that if he WAS, he'd be able to do the following WITH EASE:

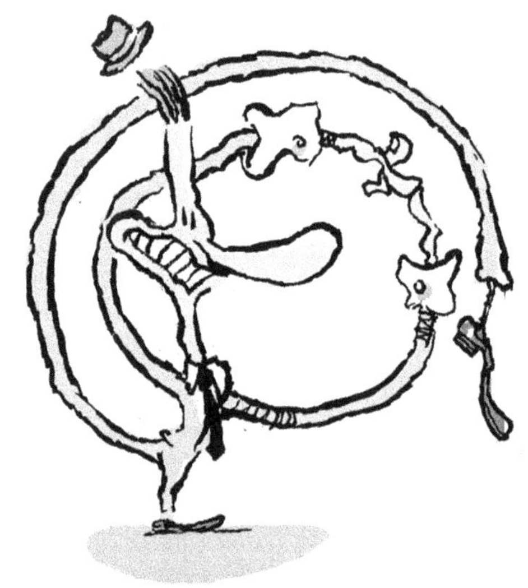

Rob Feldman's

CARTOONS, COMICS, and COWS in CARS

Margate Beach, Queensland

First Published in Australia in 2014 by COMICOZ
P.O. Box 187
MARGATE BEACH 4019
Queensland

First Edition: First Printing

Cover artwork and design, and all artwork and design within these pages by Rob Feldman www.robfeldman.com.au

Publisher, project co-ordinator, and used tea bags by Nat Karmichael www.comicoz.com

National Library of Australia Cataloguing-in-Publication entry

Author: Feldman, Robert Jacques; Author, Illustrator, Editor
Title:: Rob Feldman's Cartoons, Comics, and Cows in Cars
Robert Jacques Feldman
Writer, Illustrator, and Editor
ISBN: 9780980653526 (hardback)
Subjects: Comic books, strips, etc. -- Australian
Dewey Number: 742.5994

ACKNOWLEDGEMENTS

I wish to thank my darling wife Vicky (Na) for making it possible for me to put in all the hours, days, months, and BEYOND at the drawing board which resulted in the book being born. Big thanks to my awesome children, as well as to all of my big extended family AND to my friends for their encouragement over YEARS. Thanks to my dear sister Celia, always supportive and inspirational! Whopping thanks to Nat Karmichael of COMICOZ for suggesting the project and for giving invaluable technical and other guidance during the creation of the book. Thanks in heaps to Tony Lopes, award-winning cartoonist of INSANITY STREAK fame for providing the opportunity for my Fridge-dweller comic strips (featured in the book) to have a roaring season in selected Rural Press newspapers, and for his bountiful gems of advice. Thanks also to fellow-members of the Australian Cartoonists Association, the Australian Society of Authors, AND the Bunker Cartoon Gallery folk, all of whose company continues to inspire. Big shout out to my good friend, illustrator and painter extraordinaire Linda Adair for instructing me in the ways of the Photoshop Jedi. Appreciation to amigo mio Pablo Hernandez for his ever spot-on advice, and for the quality photography for the book and website. Thanks also to Justin, Mike, Mike, and Rich for crucial Para-tech support. Danke to our foreign language proof-readers, Katje, Ken, and Dima. And my versions of foreign languages are NOT easy to proof-read. Thanks everyone who got behind the book's Pozible crowd-funding campaign, to get 'COWS in CARS' off the ground. SPECIAL THANKS to Lindsay Foyle, Steve Little, Neville Craig Bain, Robert Price, Brian McDonald, and Bruce N Morgan for their major contributions. And ALMOST last, but certainly NOT LEAST, a BIG THANK YOU to YOU the READER, without whom this book would go completely unread by YOU the READER. And to anyone I've accidentally missed the opportunity to acknowledge here, and to all above-mentioned as well, I shall call you 'Spartacus.' And next time we meet you MAY want to greet me with: "I am Spartacus!" and I shall say, "No! I am Spartacus!", or "REALLY?! I was sure I was Spartacus!!!" And we shall laugh together for it shall be our little joke, which we shall enjoy greatly and we shall bond over it.

FOR CLARE AND JACQUES

my parents, my friends

A long time ago now, when I was a younger person (sometime before last Thursday) I learnt that Life is full of Bitter Disappointments. I somehow had perceptions that, for example, bankers were fat and jolly, rubbish collectors were smelly, and that vagrants could not be trusted. I don't know from where these biases emanated (perhaps from reading too many comics?), but I do know I had trouble dispelling those myths made from my mind while growing up.

Since that time I have met many cartoonists and artists. Each one of them had their own individual quirks, with different methods and styles used in expressing their craft. Over the years I have become both enamoured with and an advocate for Australian comic artists, believing that many of them have slaved over their works with little public recognition and even lesser acclaim.

In 2011, after too long an absence from the Australian Cartoonists' Association (which had more to do with personal reasons, rather than any disillusionment with the collective), I returned to attend the Annual Workshop and Dinner. Within the crowd of attendees at the Workshop was a man who sat attentively listening, occasionally drawing, and engaging with some of the other guests. I sat gob-smacked: this man was the **absolute personification** of my youthful perception of *what a cartoonist should **look** like!*

It wasn't until just before the last Workshop of the year, in the company of cartoonist Gary Clark, that I met **Rob Feldman.** After some superficial conversation, Gary and I were tentatively asked if we would be interested in viewing some of Rob's comics and cartoons. I have to admit that up until that moment, there had only been two new cartoonists' works whose humour and illustrative techniques impressed me from the get-go: Gary Clark and Bill Watterson. Still, I had never turned down an opportunity to view a cartoonists' work, so I wasn't about to do so then.

I was gob-smacked a second time! Rob Feldman's craft was the **absolute personification** of my youthful perception of *how comic humour should **flow**!* The fact he was unpublished boggled my mind! How could Rob's talent be hidden from all of us for so long? How could this humour be kept from being shared with as many people as possible? I had to ask him if he would allow my publishing arm **(Comicoz)** to publish his first book. I am truly honoured that he agreed.

For reasons too complicated (and silly) to explain, I have written the words to this Introduction without so far reading one page of this book. I doubt that any page contained within this book's pages will disappoint. Why *should* Life be full of Bitter Disappointments? Why *can't* Life be full of Glorious Opportunity? I believe this book will be the **absolute personification** of my youthful perceptions of *what a **comic book** should be!* Read it and see: I'll be Disappointed if you don't agree....

Nat Karmichael,
Comicoz Publisher.

Margate, September 2013.

Prologue to the Actual Introduction Page

HELLO, gentle reader (oh, alright, AND HELLO to you too, the 'Rough 'n' Tumble' reader as well!) I am SO GLAD you could make it. I don't EXACTLY know WHAT you could make - perhaps a handy BIRD-FEEDER Ⓐ or an attractive backyard GRANNY FLAT Ⓑ - but WHATEVER it was, I'm certainly GLAD you could make it.

HOW TO USE THIS BOOK

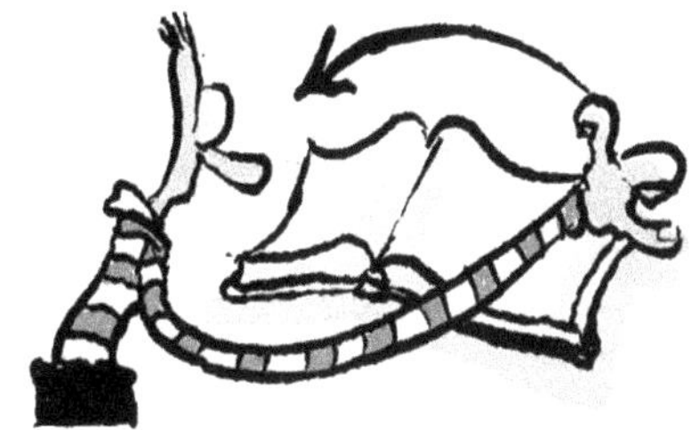

Simply READ the book from LEFT to RIGHT, and also manually TURN the PAGES' (in the time-honoured 'RIGHT-to-LEFT' motion as popularised by Zimmerman, McGee and Nguyen) which will, as a RESULT, reveal the NEXT TWO pages to be read (and so on and so forth)

The ACTUAL Introduction Page

Well, hello there, AGAIN!!

Say, would you like to gleefully PLUNGE headlong into the Wonderful World of SWASHBUCKLING Cartoonists, and TEMERARIOUS* Comic Artists?

Would you just LOVE to see A LOT of ACTUAL pages of Thigh-Slappin', Foot-Stompin', CARTOON and COMIC Adventure-Suspense-Action...um...TOMFOOLERY Fun?

Hmmm? I THOUGHT so! Well, join us NOW as we get the ball rolling with... →

* Yes! TEMERARIOUS is an ACTUAL WORD. Who knew?!

chapter 1.

everything you wanted to know about cartoonists but were afraid to and so on and so forth

CARTOONISTS - AN INTRODUCTION

As a CARTOONIST I am CONSTANTLY being approached on the street by people and other such MEMBERS of the PUBLIC, asking me probing CARTOONIST-RELATED questions such as:

Are you REALLY a CARTOONIST?

Is it TRUE that CARTOONING is one of the most PUNISHING and PHYSICALLY DEMANDING professions in the WHOLE, WIDE WORLD?

Is CARTOONING in fact considered to be the 'WWF*' of the ART WORLD'?

Is the CAPITAL of BRUNEI actually BUNDAR SERI BEGAWAN?

Do you, like, work out?

Are you, like, a MODEL or something? OMG, you TOTES should be!

TO THESE QUESTIONS I ANSWER:

Yes, Yes, No, Yes, No, Yes...

in no particular order.

In the following pages we will bring you the ANSWERS to the BURNING QUESTIONS about CARTOONISTS that have DOGGED & PLAGUED you, and in your more DESPERATE MOMENTS have KEPT YOU AWAKE at nights. NOW, FINALLY, and JUST FOR YOU, we LIFT the LID on the MYSTERIOUS WORLD of CARTOONISTS*

* Brought to you in SOPHISTICATED 'QUESTION-and-ANSWER' format.

What are the 4 Major Cartoon Groups?

THE 4 MAJOR CARTOON GROUPS ARE:

1 ANCIENT SHAOLIN MARTIAL ARTS CARTOONING

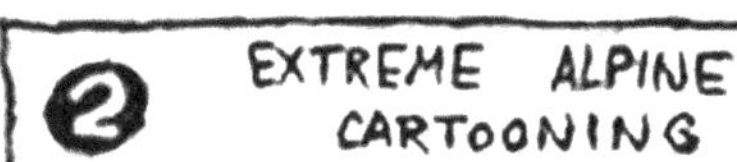

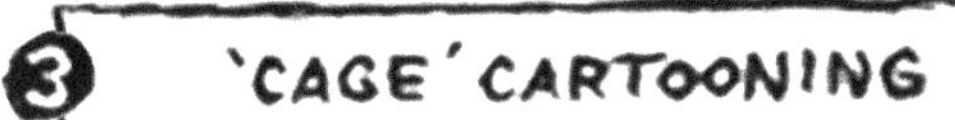

What would you say is the **BIGGEST PROBLEM** facing the **MODERN CARTOONIST**?

I'd say, without a doubt, it's Paparazzi.

Is it true that **CARTOONISTS** must have **ROCK HARD ABS** and **PECS of STEEL**?

Yes, this is true. Here ⇨ you can see a **TYPICAL CARTOONIST** doing a **RIGOROUS WORKOUT**, paying particular attention to his Upper Body Strength.

ADVERTISEMENT

HEY, READER! Ever wanted to have the BODY OF A CARTOONIST but NEVER THOUGHT YOU COULD? WELL, NOW you CAN with the NEW CARTOON-o-MATIC PEC-PUMPER PRO!!

THAT'S RIGHT! With the CARTOON-o-MATIC PEC-PUMPER PRO™ you'll get NOT ONE, NOT TWO, but THREE AMAZINGLY IMPRESSIVE CARTOON-DRAWING ARM-BULGES on your PECS!!

WANT PROOF?! This AUTHENTIC PEC-BULGE SIMULATION (above) SPEAKS FOR ITSELF!!

Available NOW at all leading CARTOON-MACHINERY-AND-BODYBUILDING-EQUIPMENT retailers.

WE ALL KNOW THAT CARTOONISTS ARE A HARDWORKING FOLK. DO CARTOONISTS EVER GET A HANKERIN' FOR A HOLIDAY?

The OFFICIAL GUIDE to CARTOONISTS on HOLIDAY*

* DUE TO OVERWHELMINGLY POSITIVE READERSHIP RESPONSE WE WILL CONTINUE TO USE THE GROUNDBREAKING 'QUESTION and ANSWER' FORMAT FOR THIS OFFICIAL GUIDE.

DO YOU HAVE A SPECIAL FEATURE PAGE SHOWING A CARTOONIST ON A TRAIN TO THE SEASIDE, AND ANOTHER CARTOONIST FROLICKING AT THE BEACH?

What are the chances?!! Yes, we DO!

BELOW: A CARTOONIST TRAVELLING BY TRAIN TO THE SEASIDE

BELOW: ANOTHER CARTOONIST **AT** THE SEASIDE.

SPOTTED ON THE SAND! The 'WHO'S WHO' OF CELEBRITY CARTOONISTS TURNING HEADS at the BEACH.

Alpha Cartoonist Alonzo McGee is completely at home in the water. And he's just as passionate about his role as a Volunteer Beach Lifeguard as he is about drawing his hilarious cartoons.

Even though on holiday, Doug Thfuffner, Head Cartoonist for 'CHEESE 'n' TOAST MONTHLY, sees the beach as a great non-cartooning enterpreneurial opportunity.

Here's Abe Ziffle whose cartoons in the Dry Rock Ridge Stockyards Gazette never fail to raise a chuckle.

Freelance cartoonist Barry Fnurtz spends HOURS at the beach for MONTHS AT A TIME waiting for his cartoon inspirations to strike, but his readers all agree that it's well worth the wait.

WHAT WOULD BE THE NUMBER ONE CARAVANNING TIP FROM CARTOONIST CARAVANNING ENTHUSIASTS ?

It would be this one

THE SUCCESS OF THE CARAVANNING EXPERIENCE IS ENTIRELY DEPENDENT ON ACHIEVING THE CORRECT CAR-WEIGHT / CARAVAN-WEIGHT RATIO.

PLEASANT CARAVANNING EXPERIENCE

② INCORRECT CAR-WEIGHT / CARAVAN WEIGHT RATIO RESULTING IN HIGHLY UNPLEASANT CARAVANNING EXPERIENCE.

DO CARTOONISTS HAVE FASCINATING ANCESTRAL HISTORIES INVOLVING A BICYCLE AND THE QUEEN OF ROMANIA?

As a rule, no, but astonishingly, in my case I DO. And here's CONCLUSIVE, UNDENIABLE PROOF.

2

The QUEEN of ROMANIA brings conciliatory FLOWERS to Great, Great, Great Uncle Constantin in hospital.

(Names have been changed to protect innocent cartoon people currently under the protection of the Cartoon People Witness Protection Program.)

3 Great, Great, Great, Great UNCLE VALENTIN owns the FIRST MOTORCYCLE in ROMANIA.

4

The FIRST MOTORCYCLE in ROMANIA EXPLODES with Great, Great, Great Great Uncle Valentin on it.

5 Assorted pieces of Great, Great, Great, Great UNCLE VALENTIN collectively become the FIRST ROMANIAN COSMONAUT in SPACE

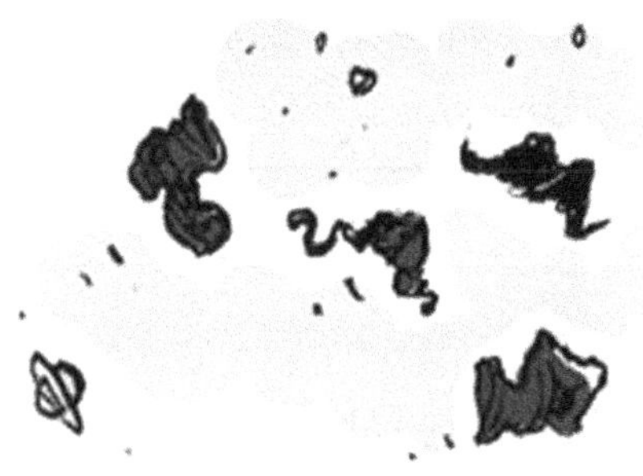

NOTE: As the very GRAPHIC DEPICTION of Great (x4) Uncle Valentin IN ORBIT is a no doubt DISTURBING one, we now bring you a SOOTHING PASTORAL SCENE...

And now back to our feature...

HAVE ANY CARTOONISTS EVER BEEN KNOWN TO HAVE MADE ANY ACTUAL CONSTRUCTIVE CONTRIBUTION TO SOCIETY?

Oh yes indeed.

Cartoonist Legend Dieter Duffelkoatzer, Editorial Cartoonist for the Dusseldorffer Daily, came across an extremely tired-looking Dachshund on the streets of Dortmund.

THE REST IS HISTORY.

WHO IS THE 'CARTOON PERSON BACHELOR OF THE YEAR'?

WHO IS THE CARTOONIST'S CARTOONIST?

Good question. Thank you for asking.

ALONZO McGEE HAS BEEN DESCRIBED AS 'The CARTOONIST's CARTOONIST' ALTHOUGH THIS CLAIM HAS RECENTLY BEEN DISCREDITED.

The CARTOONIST's CARTOONIST is, in fact, MBOKO MBOKOMBOKOMBWAKALELE, the STAFF CARTOONIST with 'The BOTSWANA BUGLE' →

HOWEVER, AS IT TURNS OUT, ALONZO McGEE IS (BY FAR) MBOKO MBOKOMBOKOMBWAKALELE's FAVOURITE CARTOONIST, THUS MAKING ALONZO McGEE OFFICIALLY 'The CARTOONIST'S CARTOONIST'S CARTOONIST'

ALPHA CARTOONIST ALONZO McGEE AT THE DRAWING BOARD.

LITERALLY.

WHAT ARE THE CUTTING-EDGE, STATE-OF-THE-ART, HI-TECH MATERIALS USED BY THE MODERN CARTOONIST?

These are what.

← A MODERN PENCIL-ACCESSORY INNOVATION: ERASER / RUBBER CLEVERLY ATTACHED TO THE END OF THE PENCIL. (I know, right?!!)

↑ A PENCIL

← A 'REAM' OF 'TYPING PAPER' [SIZE A4]

A MODERN 'GEL' PEN

A 'PERMANENT' MARKER, GREAT FOR THOSE LARGE AREAS OF BLACK.

HAVE ANY CARTOONISTS DRAWN CARTOONS ABOUT THE BIRTH OF ABRAHAM LINCOLN?

WOULD YOU HAPPEN TO HAVE A CLASSIC COMIC·DRAWING TUTORIAL BY A LEGENDARY SOVIET HERO CARTOONIST?

Я не могу найти
ключи от машины

Я вижу много тракторов. Есть,
безусловно, много тракторов

две пары
белых носков,
три фуфайки
один литр
молока

CONGRATULATIONS you the 'freshly-initiated-into-the-ways-of-the-Cartoonist' READER. You now know ABSOLUTELY EVERYTHING there is to KNOW about the
WONDERFUL...
WORLD OF
CARTOONISTS
Join us, won't you, as we turn to...

chapter 2.

cart oons & com ic s

WELCOME Please Do TO THE ACTUAL 'CARTOONS 'n' COMICS' Section of the BOOK

Here you will find, EXCLUSIVELY, a FOOT-STOMPIN', THIGH-SLAPPIN' array of COMICS and CARTOONS, from subjects as diverse as SUMO WRESTLERS and SQUEEGEE MAN to FRIDGE BOY FROM SPACE, and MONGOLIAN FERRETS. You'll TRAVEL to FARAWAY EXOTIC LOCATIONS such as GDANSK* and CESSNOCK.* You'll THRILL to the sounds of POWDERED WIGS and ELVIS SHINTARO. You'll MARVEL as you take your place on a REAL SIMULATED dentist chair. You'll LITERALLY ROLL ON THE FLOOR LAUGHING.

as you DISCOVER MAFIOSI TURNED GOOD, and

MUCH, MUCH MORE.!!

---

* Unless you already LIVE in these places in which case they won't really strike you as being all THAT exotic.

FIRST CAB off the RANK it's our JAPANESE Feature Editor KENTO SHENTOBENTO-YOSHIOMYGOSHI bringing you the ORIGINAL 1957 CLASSIC `ALL-IN-JAPANESE´ Private Eye DETECTIVE SAMURAI Ninja Monster THRILLER ACTION MYSTERY Pseudo MANGA CLASSIC...

ELVIS SHINTARO

SAMURAI DETECTIVE

アのドテ人ぺの… てつとケスウ… ヨトのアホつ…

ヲも丁の!
ワヨバ!
ズのアニ☺
もトヨべ由
...
...
...
...
のレと!
まのド

の互人り... べヨ人同... ウのてが!

ンズフ!
ヨのズイと~の
コズ生のテイ
ヨのズイと~の
コズ生のテイ
ンズはなる
るりてニ
おウの同
ヨのテ回由アコトイ夫3ズのもド
ドレミ

We interrupt the NAIL-BITING excitement of 'ELVIS SHINTARO - SAMURAI DETECTIVE' to bring you an EXCLUSIVE ALL-SUMO Double Page Single Panel Action Cartoon Series Spread...

The 'IT MAY NEVER CATCH ON' Series

SYNCHRONISED SUMO SWIMMING

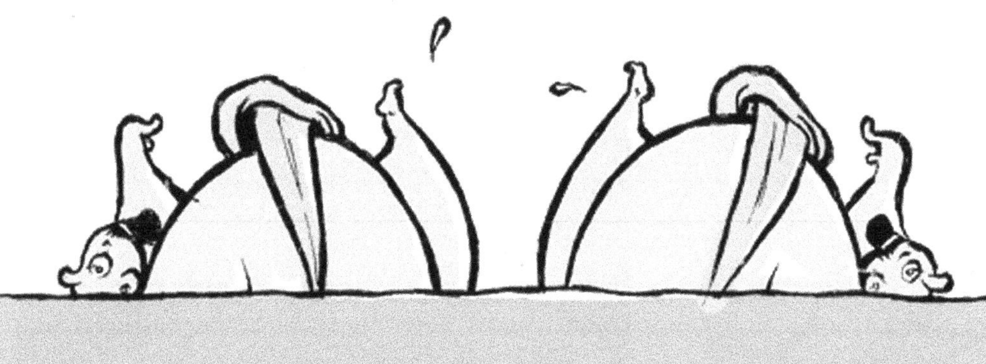

Kentaro REFUSED to let his glaringly obvious physical limitations get in the way of his all-consuming ambition to become the GREATEST GRAND WORLD SUMO CHAMPION OF ALL TIME...

The SUMO WRESTLERS HALL OF FAME
KENTO AND HIS PRECISION FORMATION SUMO STUNT MOTORCYCLE TEAM

The SUMO WRESTLERS HALL OF FAME
- SHO - UNDISPUTED SUMO 'BUNGEE-KING'
1977 - 2007

THE 'It-May-Not Catch-On' Series
FLY-WEIGHT SUMO Wrestling

Boy, Kenji has really let himself go...

Now that you've successfully met your Yearly Sumo Cartoon Quota, we can return with glee to the EDGE-OF-YOUR-SEAT EPIC DRAMA that is... ELVIS SHINTARO-SAMURAI DETECTIVE!

ズのアニ☺
もトヨベ由
ルルルル
ルルルル

のトズコテイと
ズのアニ☺

のトズコテイと
EAT AT Haburashi DINER
SUSHI·ON·A·STICK
テヨのツ
MISO·BURGERS
ブのテとよ人
ウの人
...

まのド

...

のブ人井ま!....

てつとケスウ

TO BE CONTINUED

ONE DAY

AND NOW, because we care, we bring you our **VERY OWN EXTREMELY SMART PERSON**, and **SPACE** and **SCIENCE** EDITOR, Professor Sven Øeskerdøeskerschmøesker-ersk.

Thank you Bob. Well, reading about ELVIS SHINTARO got me thinking about THRILLING OUTER-SPACE, SCI-FI EPIC ADVENTURES.
(Don't ask me why. It's just what I do)
One thought led to another, and before I knew it I was thinking about my FAVOURITE SCI-FI, ACTION-FIGURE HERO...

FridgeBoy from Space

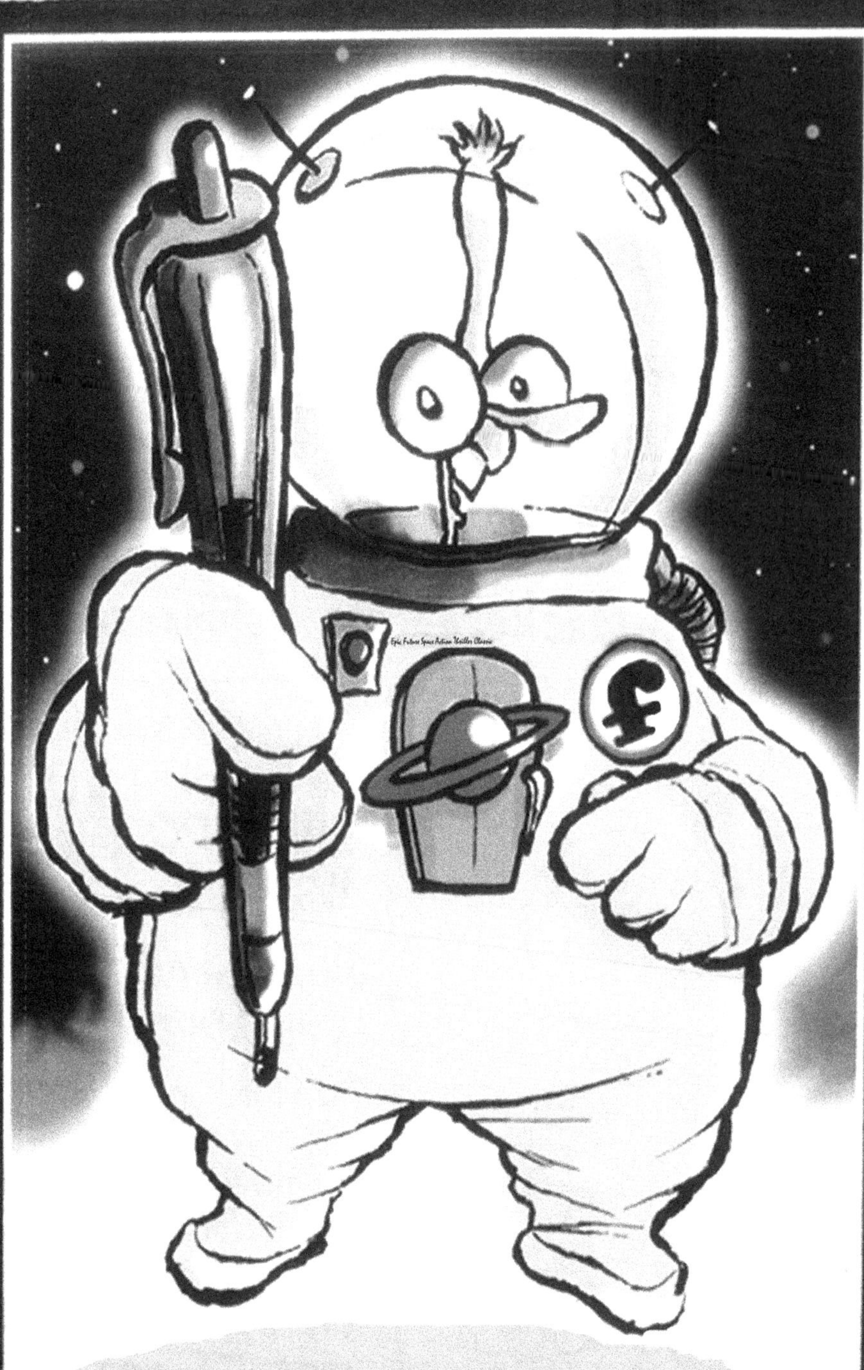

Epic Future Space Action Thriller Classic

Note: For our more contemplative reader, and in order to make the full effect of the the title REALLY SINK IN, the title is repeated below AT NO EXTRA COST to you reader.

Fridge Boy From Space!

FUTURE CLASSIC COMIC STRIP

THE BEGINNINGS

I MEAN YOU COULD ALWAYS TRY GOOGLE EARTH BUT, YOU KNOW, GOOD LUCK WITH THAT

WE INTERRUPT THE ACTION TO BRING YOU A BREAKING COMMENT FROM **THE TIMES'** RETRO SCI-FI COMIC LITERARY CRITIC, LARS PILLAGER-PLUNDERBJØRK.

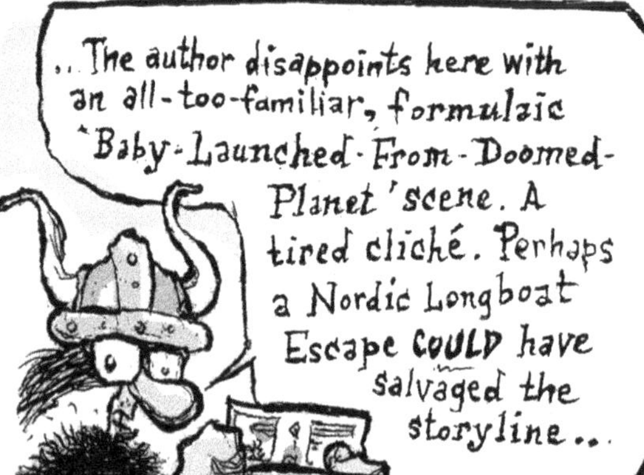

BACK TO THE ACTION..
AM I THERE YET?
MEANWHILE, DOWN ON EARTH IN A RUSTIC, RURAL SETTING THAT IS JUST BEGGING TO BE PAINTED BY SOME ARTIST...
SO ANYWAYS, THERE WAS AN ENGLISHMAN, AN IRISHMAN, AND A SCOTSMAN...
WAH HA! HA! HA! THESE ONES ALWAYS CRACK ME UP! GO ON...!

SUDDENLY
WRROAR!
WHOA!!! WHAT'S THAT?!!!
IT'S... IT'S A UFLO!
MAYDAY! MAYDAY!
AN UNIDENTIFIED FRIDGE-LIKE OBJECT!!
CRASH!

...INCOMING, APPARENTLY, FROM OUTER SPACE...

...CRASHED IN OUR CORN FIELD!!
I TOLD you if you build it they will come...
LOOK!... A CRATER!!
CORN FIELDS

WHA?...
IT'S...
KEVIN KOSTNER!!!

HOLD IT RIGHT THERE, MISTER!!!
ENOUGH with the whole 'If-you-build-it-they-will-come-Kevin-Kostner' thing!
POKE!
The Artist
Let's try that again
WHA?...
IT'S...
A CUTE LITTLE BABY!!!
Goo!

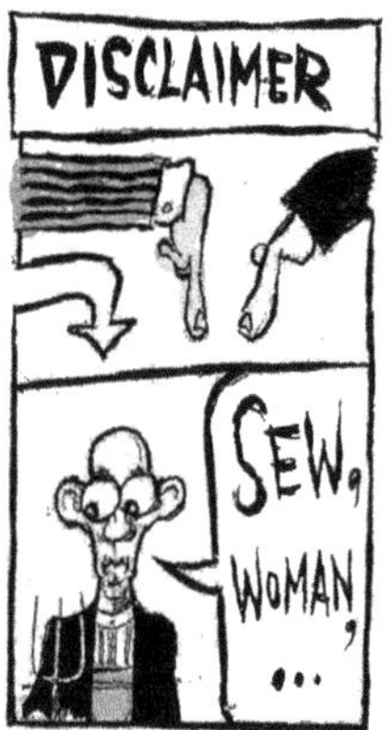

In reference to the **SEWING MACHINE** scene, the artist wishes to state that he would **NEVER** address a woman as '**WOMAN**,' nor would he expect her to do **ALL** the 'Alien-Friendly-Space-Suit'-Sewing all by herself.

The artist used the word 'Woman' as in "Sew, Woman" **ONLY** in the interests of **HISTORICAL ACCURACY** as it does reflect the **QUAINT**, yet alarmingly **POLITICALLY INCORRECT** attitudes of the era.

We shall raise you as our own, normal in every way...

..AND WE SHALL CALL YOU FRIDGE BOY...
FOR NOW HE SHALL BE CALLED FRIDGE BOY

...FOR YOU CAME TO US IN A SPACE CRAFT THAT WOULD, TO THE UNTRAINED EYE, LOOK REMARKABLY LIKE A FRIDGE.

AND WE SHALL ALSO CALL YOU FRIDGE BOY IN HONOUR OF THE GREAT DOUGAL MacFRIDGE, LEGENDARY CELTIC LEGEND...

..AND THE FIRST PERSON OF SCOTTISH PERSUASION TO TRAVEL INTO OUTER SPACE..

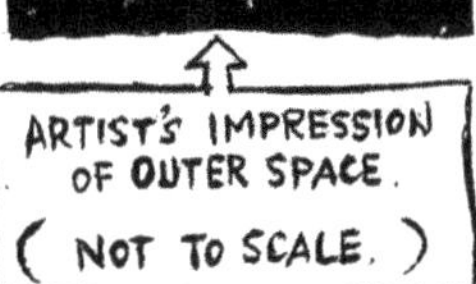
ARTIST'S IMPRESSION OF OUTER SPACE.
(NOT TO SCALE.)

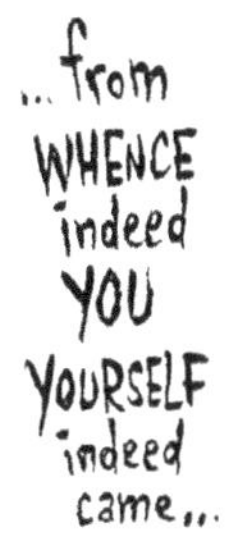
...from WHENCE indeed YOU YOURSELF indeed came...

It all happened in the GREAT SCOTTO-ENGLO Wars of 1296 - PRESENT
..when the SCOTS beseiged the ENGLISH in the BATTLE of LOCH OCHANAHOOTAWEE

THE ENGLISH FORTIFICATION IS ABOOT* TO COLLAPSE...
ONE MORE CATAPULTED BOULDER, AND VICTORY WILL BE OURS!...
*about

But we've run OOTA* BOULDERS!!
!
McHuh?!
*out of

It was to be the moment of DOUGAL MacFRIDGE'S DATE with DESTINY!...

I'LL BE YOUR CATAPULT BOULDER!!
...FOR I'LL NO' HAVE it said that any son of Angus MacFRIDGE-McGee-MacDougal canna OCH AN' AWEE AN'A HOOT AN'A HIGH ROAD and an OCH and a WEE!!..

What's he saying, Dougal?
It doesn't MATTER, Dougal. Clearly, MacFRIDGE is the man for the job!!!

AND SO DOUGAL MacFRIDGE STEPPED FORWARD AND THEN SPOKE THE WORDS THAT HAVE ECHOED DOWN THROUGH HISTORY...

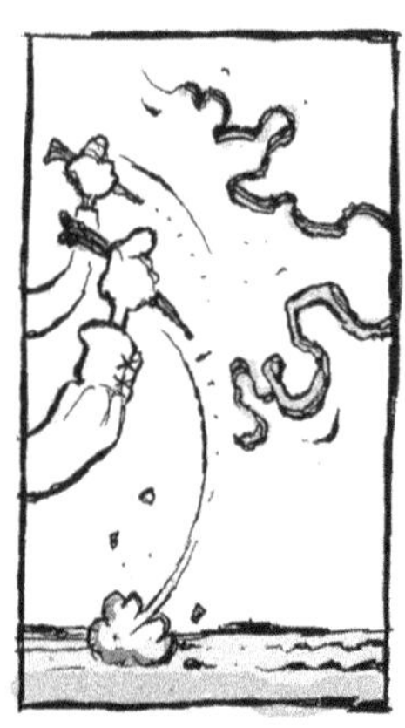

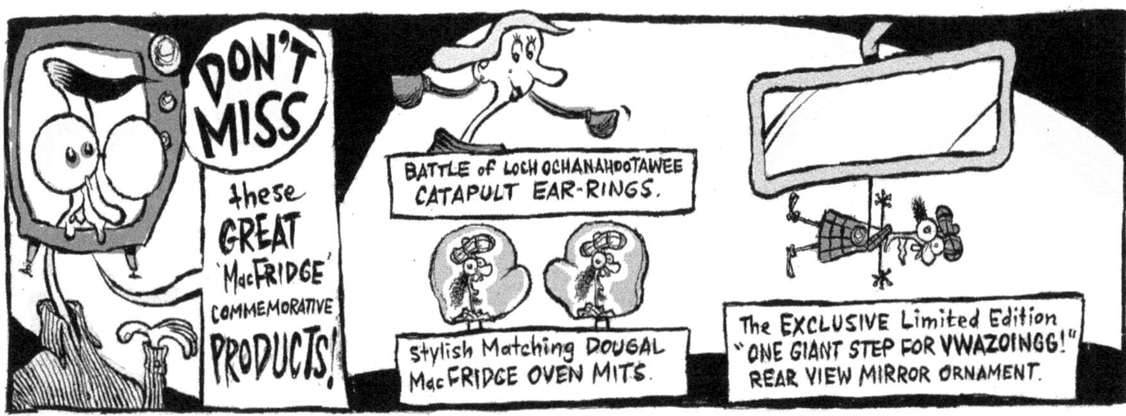

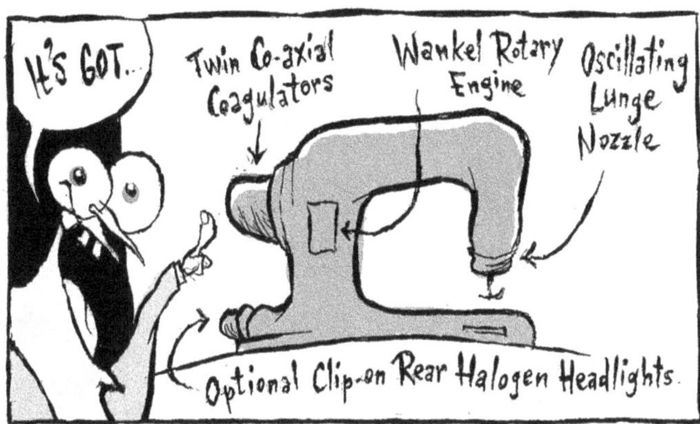

HURRY! ONLY WHILE SOCKS LAST!

DON'T MISS the NEXT EPISODE of FRIDGE BOY from SPACE

Hey Kids! It's time for your VERY OWN, not ONE, but TWO cartoons about **SPACE and BEYOND!**

A HIGHLY TECHNOLOGICAL LOOK AT
MODERN TECHNOLOGY

email shmeemail!

Modern Motoring Phenomenon:
GPS Rage
KEEP LEFT. KEEP LEFT. STAY IN THE LEFT LANE. NOW.. SHARP TURN RIGHT!..
I HATE YOU!
I HATE YOU!
I HATE YOU!
I HATE YOU!!..
CRUNCH!
CRUNCH!

THE DAWN OF
SOCIAL MEDIA

Face-book
The Early Days
Gronkk adds Uggnk as a friend on his Facebook cave.

Early Face-book
"Poking"
Krurrgh has poked you: Poke back.
POKE!
POKE!

Twitter
Early, cave Version
Grurgg and Krunkk on Twitter.
TWEET! TWEET! TWEET! TWEET! TWEET!
Translation:
"I am squeezing this little bird."

SPECIAL Technological Advancement INVENTORS Supplement

As you very well know, it has been said:

'Build a Better MOUSETRAP and People Will BEAT a PATH to YOUR DOOR'

And SPEAKING of 'MOUSETRAPS', GERMANY has mousetraps. Cue our GERMAN Feature Editor, Klaus Gugelhupf, who proudly brings you...

or Der Deutscher Phrase GeBooken für Das Grosse Über Pocket

Welcome to GERMANY (arguably the MOST GERMAN of all of the European countries)

BUT WHAT'S THIS?!! YOU CAN'T SPEAK GERMAN?!!

Well, DON'T WORRY!!! With this handy VERY LARGE POCKET GERMAN PHRASE BOOK you'll be SPEAKING GERMAN FLUENTLY *in minutes*!!!

The Results Speak for Themselves.

This GERMAN PHRASE BOOK may contain traces of ACTUAL GERMAN

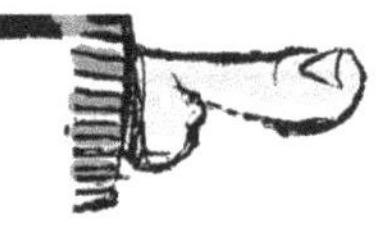

Forword

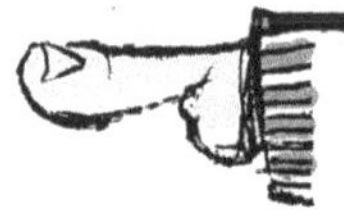

by Otto Zwischenzimmeraugenblick

Forward, Borussia Mönchengladbach FC

(Oh, Ha! Ha! A 'Foreword' written by a 'Foreward.' PRICELESS!)

"Unencumbered by any actual working knowledge of German, Rob Feldman is able to bring a fresh, unbiased approach to the German language... I highly commend this German Phrasebook to you."

Epilogue to the Forward

Congratulations!

You are holding in your hands the 1,000,000th copy of the Very Large Pocket German Phrase Book (Soon to be translated into English under the title 'The Very Large Pocket ENGLISH Phrase Book.)

The OTHER almost 999,999-ish 'UNITS' of 'The VERY LARGE POCKET GERMAN PHRASEBOOK' are currently being stored in the Geschitzelschmitznitz GERMAN PHRASEBOOK WAREHOUSE-HAUS in Baden-Baden just past the Frauleinweiss-garberhofplatz TURN OFF on Autobahn Achtundzwanzigsieben undneununddreiundfünf. You can't miss it.

Useful Phrases

of Significant Usefulness.

Wir haben große Eile

We're in a terrible hurry.

Was für Beschwerden haben Sie?

What seems to be the problem?

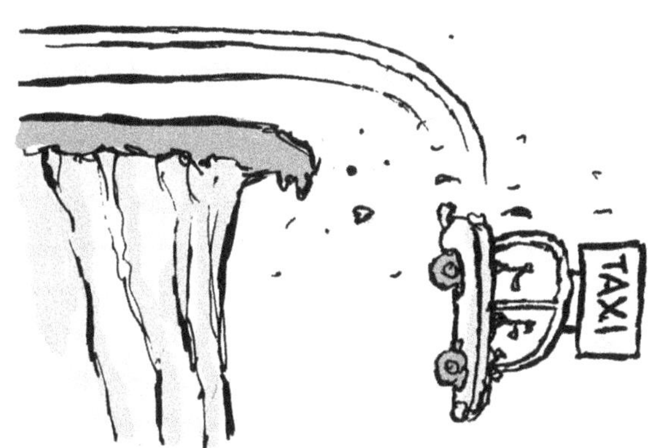

Könnten wir vielleicht einen anderen Weg nehmen?

Could we possibly take another route?

Herr Ober, mein Steak ist gar nicht durch.

Waiter, my steak is underdone.

Herr Ober, kann ich bitte den Schnabel?

Waiter, could I have the bill please?

Useful Vocabulary

Der Schlagsahnescheiben-wischerselbsloser

Shaving-Cream Windscreen-Wiper Self-Timer

Die Zuverlassigkranken-schwesternasentropfen

Reliable Nurse Nose-Drops

Der Herrlichüberober-ausgezeichnetskihose

Wonderful Head-Waiter Excellent Ski-Pants

CONVERSATION

1. At a Restaurant

Inge and Wolfgang are enjoying a meal of Deutschersausage and Sauerkraut as Inge gets to the punchline of an excellent Bavarian joke.

Inge: ... **und dann sagt er: "Du hast Deine Lederhosen verkehrtrum an!"**

(... and then he said, "Your leather breeches are on back to front!")

Wolfgang: **Oh, ha! ha! ha! ha! ha! ha! ha!**

(Oh, ha! ha! ha! ha! ha! ha! ha!)

Inge: **Ja! LEDERHOSEN! HA! HA! HA! HA! HA!**

(Yes! LEATHER BREECHES! HA! HA! HA! HA! HA!)

Wolfgang: **Ha! Ha! JA! JA! DU HAST DEINE LEDERHOSEN VERKEHRTRUM AN! HA! HA! HA!!**

(Ha! Ha! YES! YES! YOUR LEATHER BREECHES ARE ON BACK TO FRONT!! HA! HA! HA!!)

CONVERSATION

2. Introductions.

Heinrich arrives at a conference to hear a lecture by Herr Professor Wolfgang 'Call Me Wolfi' Überschnitzel of the University of Ausbeimitnachvonzuborussiamönchengladbach. There he sees Günther who introduces Heinrich to his friends.

Günther: Hallo, Heinrich!

Heinrich: Hallo, Günther!

Günther: Heinrich, dies ist (this is) Lotti, Werner, Ulrich, Klaus, Brunhilde, Mitzi, Albrecht, Guido, Edeltraud, Berta, Astrid, Leroy, Axel, Stig, Foo Foo, und Herr Professor Wolfgang Überschnitzel

Heinrich: Oh hallo Lotti, Werner, Ulrich, Klaus, Brunhilde, Mitzi, Albrecht, Guido, Edeltraud, Berta, Astrid, und (and)... er (er)... um (um)...

Günther: Leroy!

Heinrich: Oh ja! Leroy. Ha. Ha. (Oh yes! Leroy. Ha. Ha.) Hallo Leroy! Hallo Leroy und (and) Axel, Stig, Foo Foo, und (and) Herr Professor Wolfgang Überschnitzel.

End-of-Phrasebook Test (ADVANCED Level)

Translate THIS typical GERMAN Paragraph into ENGLISH

Professor Ludwig Ichweißnicht of the Deutscher Languagen Und Sprechen Und Readen Institute of VolksWagenKopf.

Der Flugzimmerhoff-hauspferd Bungee Sprung Kamelreiter in das Krankenhaus einzweidreivierfünf sechssiebenachtneun zehn oh es ist Franz Beckenbauer mit ein Überbratt-wurst und das sieht aus wie Jürgen Klinsmann lederhosen.

CONGRATULATIONS! Thanks to the VERY LARGE POCKET GERMAN PHRASEBOOK combined with your natural aptitude for languages, and your diligent study habits, YOU CAN NOW SPEAK GERMAN FLUENTLY!! So, BRAVO and WELL DONE YOU! And NOW, like MILLIONS of GERMAN-SPEAKING GERMAN Theatre-and-Cinema Goers, it is time for you to enjoy (your very own) ...

Intermission

YOU COULD...

And for those MULTI-TASKING readers among you who THRIVE on the thrill of the EXTREME, you who SPEND your INTERMISSIONS like you LIVE your LIFE, pushing yourselves through the 'BURN' to the LIMITS of HUMAN ENDURANCE, how about...

... doing **ALL FOUR THINGS AT THE SAME TIME!**

COMING SOON

ELVIS SHINTARO

MUNCH!

MUNCH!

Mmphh nggrph fmmph grrrph ...

OKAY PEOPLE! Intermission's over.
Back to your seats if you please!
For NOW it's time for...

chapter 3.

even more cartoons & comics

We can NOW REVEAL that SPECIAL HIGHLY TECHNICAL 'INTELLIGENCE-SENSORS' placed under your SEAT have INDICATED that you are an EXCEPTIONALLY CLEVER PERSON with an IQ WELL into the DOUBLE DIGIT range!! I KNOW, right?!!! And THAT qualifies you to do the PUZZLES in our EXCLUSIVE...

Hey KIDS!
Here's Some FOOT-STOMPIN' PUZZLE FUN,..
...Just for You!
1 MATCH the Tail to the Creature!
2 Can you NAME them?
Answers on Next Page

Well done, you!
You Got Them ALL RIGHT!!
THE STRING-TAILED, SPOTTED THNUKK
THE CHUNKY-TAILED, SUMMER FRIZZ-EAR.
The SQUIGGLY-TAILED, TIGER-SHNOZZLE.
THE STRIPE-TAILED, SPONGE-FERRET.

MYSTERY PICTURES

Can **YOU** tell what they are?

A.

B.

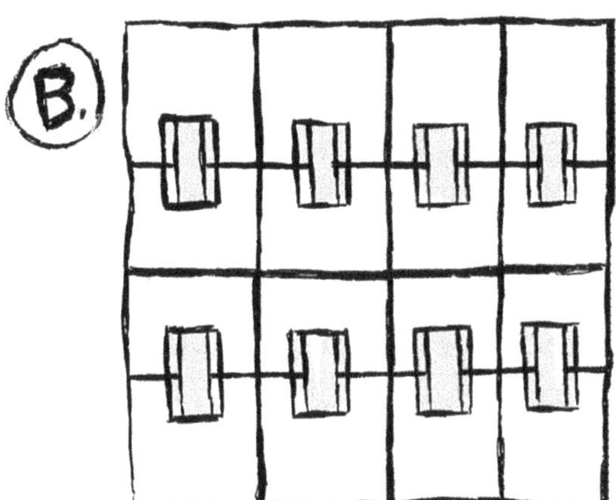

Hey Kids! Can you SPOT the **10 DIFFERENCES** *between* THIS PICTURE?

MYSTERY PICTURES *Explained*

A short person sitting behind a large-ish person at a cinema, uses a periscope to see the screen.

A youngster wearing braces.

Answers to 'SPOT THE DIFFERENCES'

But hey, GOOD TRY!!! And WELL DONE YOU! Because...

And speaking of ITALY, we proudly present our special Italian feature...

WHEN MAFIOSI turn GOOD

Arturo 'Oven Mitts' Giovaniello baking scones for the Country Women's Association Yearly Morning Tea Fundraiser

Guido 'The Babysitter' Gucci takes time out from his Day Care Centre work to man the pedestrian crossing outside the Happy Pastures Retirement Home.

Antonio 'Rotor Blades' Lopescarelli donating his time to run errands and mow Mrs. Henderson's lawn.

Salvatore 'Cotton Wool Balls' Scorsone puts himself through medical school to become a leading surgeon, specialising in Knee Cap Reconstruction Surgery.

Vincenzo 'After You Ma'am' Fogliati with his extensive collection of cement shoes and garden gnomes up for auction to raise funds for his 'Be Nice To Everyone Day' charity.

Lorenzo 'Annette' Funicello surprises members of the rival Botticelli Family in the now legendary 'Valentine's Day Roses and Chocolates Delivery'

And speaking **STILL** of Italians, did you know that Italian people made the **LAMBORGHINI** motor car? and that **LAMBORGHINI** just **HAPPENS** to be the **SURNAME** of leading Italian celebrity dentist, Dr. ENRICO LAMBORGHINI? And so, and with not inconsiderable dental hygeine related pride, we present...

EXCLUSIVELY...

DENTIST CHAIR

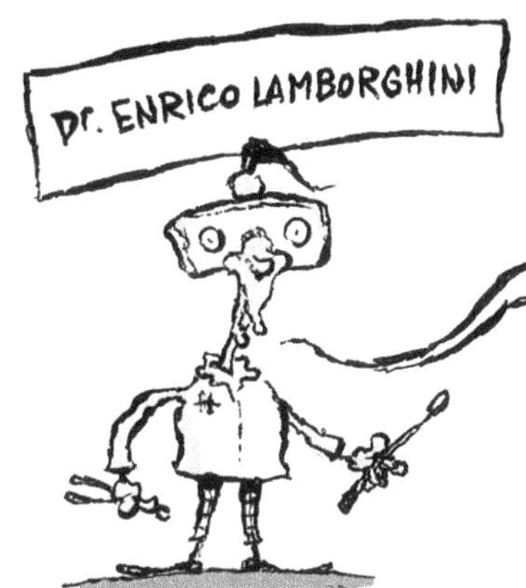

If YOU'RE anything like ME, well,...
then YOU'RE A DENTIST!!
HA! HA! HA! HA! HA!
Oh, I've got MILLIONS of them!

BUT SERIOUSLY...

Why WOULDN'T you WANT to be a DENTIST?

1 DENTISTS GET TO GO TO ALL THE COOL DENTIST ONLY PARTIES.

2 DENTISTS GET TO SAVE HUNDREDS OF DOLLARS ON THEIR OWN DENTIST BILLS

Dr. Irwin Thudmeyer doing a tricky after-hours Avuncular Incisor removal procedure.

But hey, DENTISTRY isn't ALL about UNCONTROLLABLE SALIVAL ERUPTIONS, HIGH-POWERED SPIT-SUCKER HOSES, AND NEEDLE-INDUCED FRONTAL FACE PARALYSIS

There's ANOTHER, **LESS GLAMOUROUS** side of DENTISTRY that's not often talked about.

THAT'S RIGHT! I'm talking here about the DISTURBING FACT that we DENTAL PROFESSIONALS have to deal with HUNDREDS and HUNDREDS of actual DENTAL PATIENTS...

Oh, don't get me WRONG here. The TEETH we have NO PROBLEM WITH. We can handle the TEETH.

But what we dentists STRUGGLE WITH is having to deal with DENTAL PATIENT AFTER DENTAL PATIENT -- most showing a FLAGRANT DISREGARD for their DENTAL PROFESSIONAL's FEELINGS -- who confront their DENTAL PROFESSIONAL with UNRESTRAINED, INAPPROPRIATE, and INCONSIDERATE displays of CHRONIC DENTIST CHAIR ANXIETY.

That's right. You know who I'm talking about, mister!

BUT COULD this problem REALLY be as WIDESPREAD as we're suggesting? To find out we sent our INVESTIGATIVE DENTAL CARTOONIST, Bjørn Snørkersgaaard, into a TYPICAL DENTIST's WAITING ROOM to investigate. The results of Bjørns EXCLUSIVE INVESTIGATION (his groundbreaking 'DENTAL CLINIC WAITING ROOM GALLERY - Portraits of Apprehension') speak for themselves

State-of-the-Art Drawing Equipment

DENTAL CLINIC WAITING ROOM

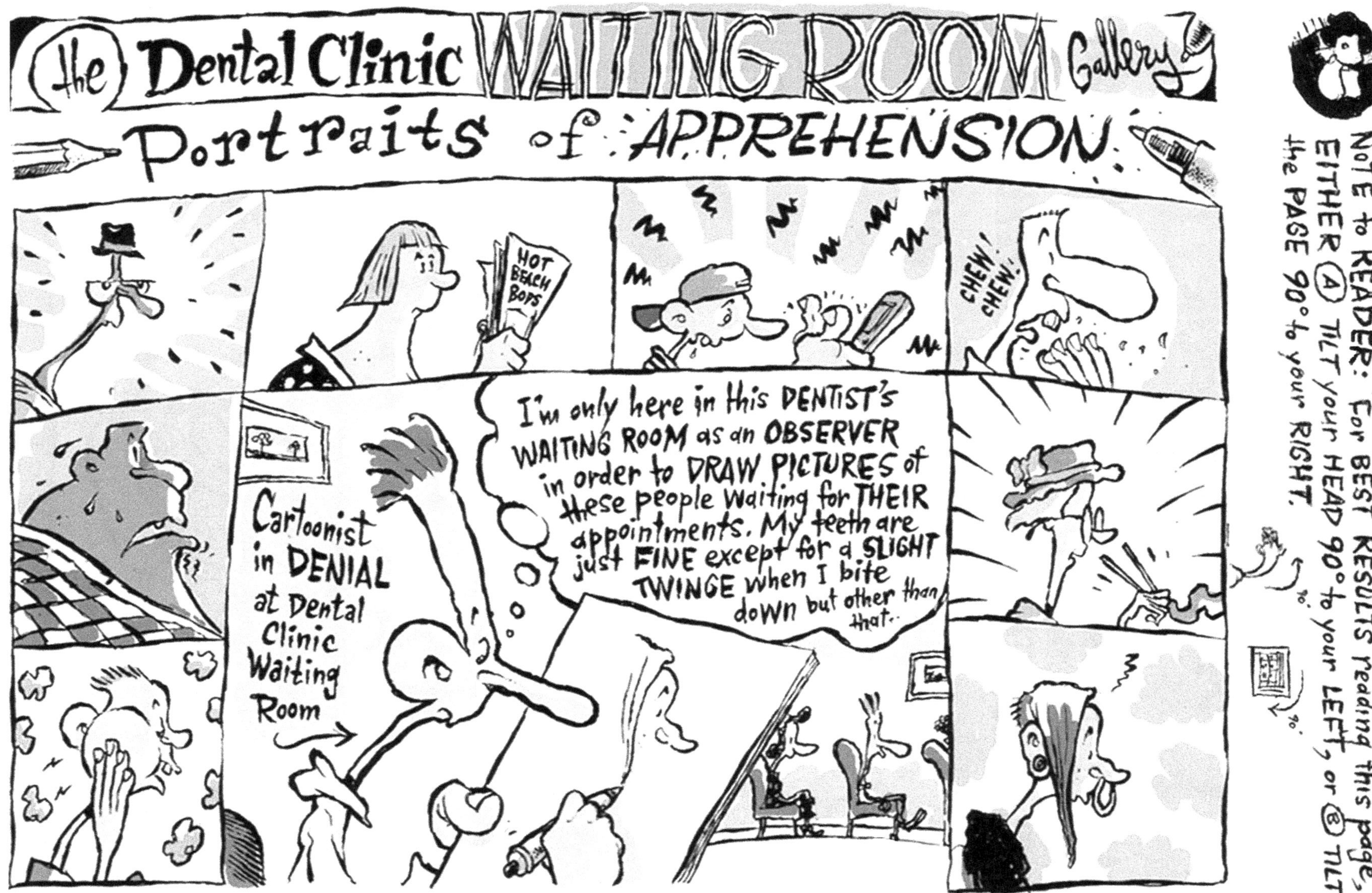

NOTE to READER: For BEST RESULTS reading this page, EITHER (A) TILT your HEAD 90° to your LEFT, or (B) TILT the PAGE 90° to your RIGHT.

But can ANYTHING be DONE to COMBAT this BLIGHT on what would OTHERWISE be your COMPLETELY UNBLEMISHED Dentist Visit RECORD?!

You can bet your MOLARS it CAN!!!

PRESENTING

Dr. Enrico Lamborghini's

STRATEGY #1

REMEMBER that the DENTIST is your FRIEND and is on YOUR SIDE!

Rose Petals being scattered by Dental Professional

STRATEGY #2

THINK CHEERY and PLEASANT FARAWAY THOUGHTS

STRATEGY #3

STRIKE UP A FRIENDLY MID-PROCEDURAL CONVERSATION with your DENTAL PROFESSIONAL

Reciting Page 252 of the Hanoi Telephone Directory.

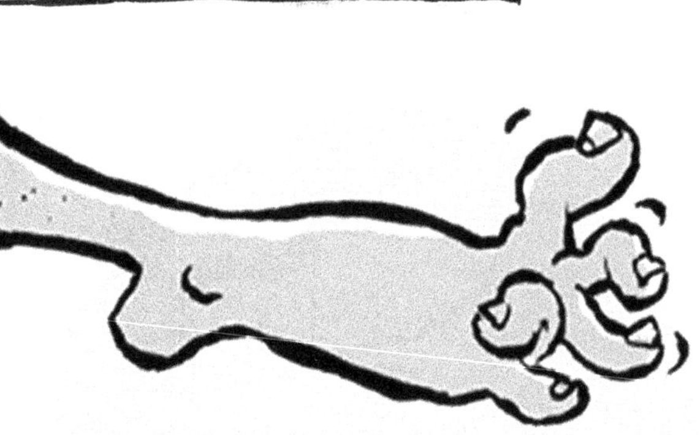

RELEASE THAT TENSION BY DOING A SERIES OF TOE YOGA-AEROBIC-TAI CHI-STRETCH-EXERCISE MANOUVRES

STRATEGY # 5

FROM YOUR PERFECT VANTAGE POINT, WHY NOT TRY COUNTING YOUR DENTAL PROFESSIONAL'S NASAL HAIRAGE?*

*Do Not Attempt This If You Have a Heart Condition.

STRATEGY # 6

HAVE A BRIEF OUT-OF-BODY EXPERIENCE*

* Don't overdo this one.

THIS COMIC HAS BEEN RECOMMENDED BY 9 OUT OF 10 DENTISTS. THE 10th DENTIST IS DR. KENJI SHOKORUKUSHINJIKINJIKENTO-BENTO, WHO IS, BELIEVE ME, **VERY** HARD TO PLEASE.

No! I DON'T recommend it, no way!

AMAZING FACT Did you know that there are MANY dentists in POLAND?

And now, in a WORLD EXCLUSIVE, we bring you

Dr. STANISLAW ZBIGNIWZZNIZZ-NOSCZEWSKINOSCZBIGNEWSKI as he PROUDLY PRESENTS

(or in POLISH: 'PAGESKI POLSKAYA')

Proudly Supported by the GDANSK SHIPYARDS.

(Motto: We have LOTS of SHIPS and they're in YARDS)

And now PLEASE to making welcome leading Polish POET, ACADEMIC, and WELDER, PAVEL ZBNYZDUMDIDUMSKI

as he sings Gdansk Shipyard's 'SHIPYARD ANTHEM'...

"OH ZDYAZK GDANSK ZNIWZIEWSKI
(oh Gdansk, oh Gdansk, oh Shipyard)
ZBIGNIZWISNIEVSKI NOSC TAK TAK
(May there be ships, many ships)
POLSKA POLSKA ZNYOSZKNYANSK"
(oh baby, yeah baby, ooh baby baby)

HERE NOW IS AN EXCLUSIVE PERSONALLY TYPED POLISH-RELATED NOTE FROM ME PERSONALLY TO YOU THE READER

Some couple of years ago in the actual, not-made-up world, I did a 7 page comic for an actual Polish international comic competition. The competition called for comics on any topic as long as no words or text were used. The comic I did, when completed, would have been a REAL CONTENDER for FIRST PRIZE had I been able to get it finished on time and thus meet the deadline. Though Poland missed it, may you enjoy...

Squeegee
Man

the End

AND NOW an IMPORTANT Squeegee-related COMMUNITY SERVICE ANNOUNCEMENT

Sadly, there are SOME PEOPLE in our community labouring under the cruel MISCONCEPTION that SQUEEGEES have no PARALLELS or COUNTERPARTS in the ANIMAL KINGDOM.

Oh, how wrong these people are.

Just let the SQUEEGEE-ANIMAL SKEPTICS take a look at THIS incontrovertible evidence...

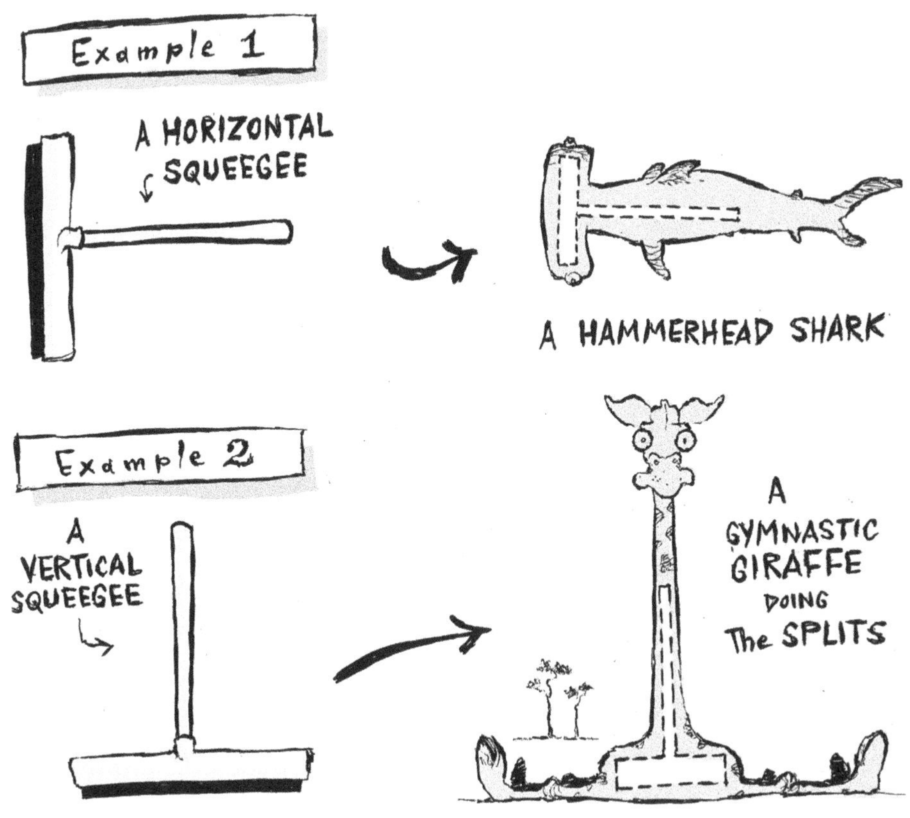

We rest our case. And speaking of SQUEEGEE-SHAPED GIRAFFES, let us now segue seamlessly into our 'once-in-a-lifetime' 'ANIMALS' feature named appropriately enough...

ANIMALS

The Elephant in the Room Gets Professional Help.
They DON'T even SEE me! And I'm RIGHT THERE IN THE ROOM with them!..

SCUBA DIVING BANTAM
The Chicken of the Sea.

An UNSUSTAINABLE Free Range Chicken farm.

And speaking of ANIMALS, SOME animals are the ACTUAL HOUSEHOLD PETS of ACTUAL SPORTSPEOPLE which brings us, not surprisingly, and some would say inevitably, to... →

THE WONDERFUL WORLD OF SPORTS

featuring

SOME TYPICAL SPORTS

TABLE TENNIS

CAGE FIGHTING

SOCCER

IGLOO-KAYAKING

GFC-INDUCED COST-CUTTING, AUSTERITY ATHLETICS EVENTS

COMBINED POLE-VAULT HURDLES

RECYCLED TOILET FLOAT HAMMER THROW

AND NOW FOR OUR SPECIAL AUSTRALIAN SPORTS FEATURE...

The Definitive GUIDE to AUSTRALIAN SPORTS

Pictured left: Australia's Rory O'Fluke bowls one of his trademark SEAM LEG-SPIN OFF-SPIN YORKER BOUNCER GOOGLIES.

It has been said that AUSTRALIA is a NATION of SPORTSMEN, SPORTSWOMEN, and EVEN SPORTSCHILDREN, and SPORTS·HOUSEHOLDPETS,

ONE OF THE MOST POPULAR AUSTRALIAN SPORTS is CRICKET [pictured ABOVE and RIGHT] which has virtually NOTHING in common with today's FEATURED AUSTRALIAN SPORT...

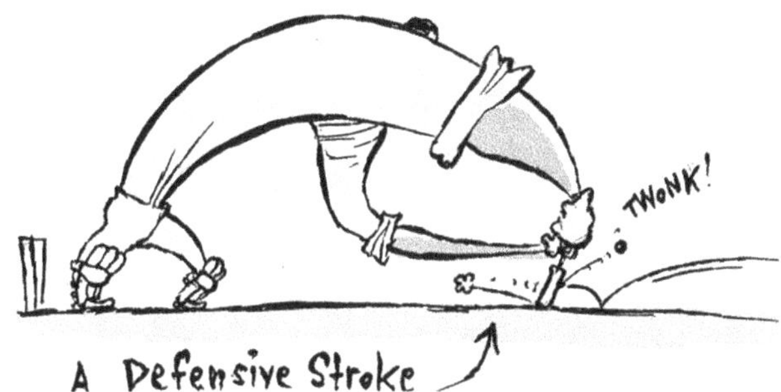

A Defensive Stroke

RUGBY LEAGUE or NRL

AND NOW → **The COMPLETE Rules**

ALL YOU WILL EVER NEED TO KNOW ABOUT THE GAME!

A TEAM of 13 PLAYERS made up of LOCKS, FIVE-EIGHTHS, HOOKERS etc does its best to run the length of a RECTANGULAR FIELD while doing highly technical moves such as OFFLOADS, DUMMIES, and REVERSE HALF HITCHES as they PASS a FOOTBALL to each other in a BACKWARDS motion until they reach a LINE at the FAR END of the field where ONE of the PLAYERS places the ball on the GROUND (PAST the line) in a clever move called a TRY at which point the PLAYER'S TEAM-MATES erupt in JUBILANT CELEBRATION at which point the TEAM converges on the TRY-SCORER for an exceptionally boisterous GROUP HUG

The TEAM is then generously awarded 4 POINTS by a trusted ADJUDICATOR or 'REFEREE' *(preeet!)* who has the unwavering RESPECT of the PLAYERS unless he should have an uncharacteristic BRAIN-FREEZE or TEMPORARY LAPSE in JUDGEMENT but that's like a TRILLION-TO-ONE against and basically NEVER HAPPENS. Immediately AFTER the TRY is AWARDED, one player is selected to KICK a the STATIONARY FOOTBALL from a fixed point x OVER a HORIZONTAL POST attached to (and between) two parallel VERTICAL POSTS which bear an uncanny resemblance to the CAPITAL LETTER 'H', and which is/are called, simply, the GOALPOSTS H. When this task is SUCCESSFULLY COMPLETED, the REFEREE, perhaps BUOYED by the POSITIVE and HEARTWARMING response to his having 'AWARDED' the previous 4 POINTS, AWARDS a further 2 POINTS. The player who has successfully kicked the ball over the LARGE METAL 'H' SHAPE, looks looks around in UNSURPRISING EXPECTATION of ANOTHER GROUP HUG, but MOMENTUM has WANED, the MOMENT has PASSED, and the PLAYER settles for POLITE CLAPPING and a PAT ON THE BACK from a passing GATORADE-IMBIBING TEAM-MATE.

CONGRATULATIONS! You now know ALL THE RULES of NRL and can confidently get out there and jolly well GIVE 110%

your very own

Picasso's 'COURT ROOM ARTIST' Period was short-lived

IN 1907 AND 1908 THE YOUNG ADOLF HITLER WAS REJECTED BY THE ACADEMY OF FINE ARTS VIENNA.

HAD HE BEEN ACCEPTED, HISTORY MAY HAVE TOLD A DIFFERENT STORY...

Sid Vicious and Johnnie Rotten visit the Art Gallery.

The UPPER TRACTORGRADSIBIRSK BIENNALE in conjunction with the MONGOLIAN NORTHERN REGIONAL GUGGENHEIM MUSEUM OF YAK HUSBANDRY AND MODERN ART

proudly present

THE CARTOONISTS WHO DEFECTED TO 'ART'

In much the way that in the WORLD OF ESPIONAGE certain SECRET AGENTS **DEFECT** to the OTHER SIDE...

or that in the WORLD OF FASHION, some TOP MODELS make the SWITCH to becoming TOP MODEL SLASH ACTORS...

so too do SOME CARTOONISTS DEFECT to 'ART.' Experience THESE fine, examples!

Sigmund Freud and the Electric Water Jug II

Otto Blahblahmeyer

(Formerly Staff Cartoonist with the Achoogesundheit Gazette)

Oils , Guache, Canvas, Belly button lint

" Inspired by a late 19th Century Viennese psychadelic psycho-analytical band of the same name, Blahblahmeyer's iconic and disturbing *Sigmund Freud and the Electric Water Jug II* courageously confronts the dream reality or perhaps the very reality of dreams themselves. Is Freud trapped IN a childhood dream as he contemplates the water jug? Or indeed is he awake yet struggling to reconcile the Ego and the Id ? Why is the water taking so darn long to boil? Did Freud forget to turn it on? If a water jug boils in the forest and no one hears it , is it really a water jug? It would need a REALLY long cord argues Freud."

Mr. Furry Man Paints

Gaston Bon-Nuit

(Formerly Chief Cartoonist with the Paris Metro Rail Illustrated Annual Timetable)

Acrylics, Oils , Fur, Crayons on Canvas

" In this emotive Self-Portrait, *Mr. Furry Man Paints* , we see a painting that was to signal an artistic revolution of sorts and that was to send shockwaves through the Cartoonist Slash Artist community nay world. With *Mr. Furry Man Paints* and its bold almost hypnotic strokes , and aggressive yet subtly nuanced furriness , Gaston Bon Nuit burst onto the scene as the founder of an entirely new Art Movement , named with stunning appropriateness , *FURRY-ISM.* Yet sadly , and as in the case of many a creative genius before him, Gaston was far, FAR ahead of his time , and he remained sadly yet perhaps inevitably , the ONLY member of the *Furry-ist* School, ever, unlike the *Pointalists* (see Seurat et al) whose adherents numbered well into the 2 or 3."

Untitled with Conductor
and Banana Skin

Aristotle Aristidelopolopolis
(Creator of popular syndicated comic strip, 'It's All Greek to Me!')

Pencil, Pen, Ink, Butcher's Paper

Aristidelopolopolis's transformation from Cartoonist into Artist came without warning as the result of a personal crisis which preceded his much anticipated Mid-Life Crisis by some six months. His then girlfriend of ten years left Aristidelopolopolis for a Trojan. Years later, and of course with the benefit of hindsight, Aristidelopolopolis would candidly tell close aquaintances that he should have been alerted to the warning signs, in particular the large wooden Trojan horse parked sometimes for hours at a time outside the apartment Aristidelopolopolis and his girlfriend shared in Athens which is in Greece. In *Untitled with Conductor and Banana Skin* Aristelop-and-so-on-and-so-forth gives us as the viewers a glimpse into this painful period of his life, and art historians have long suspected that the conductor indeed represents Aristel etc.etc. and the banana skin, the Trojan.

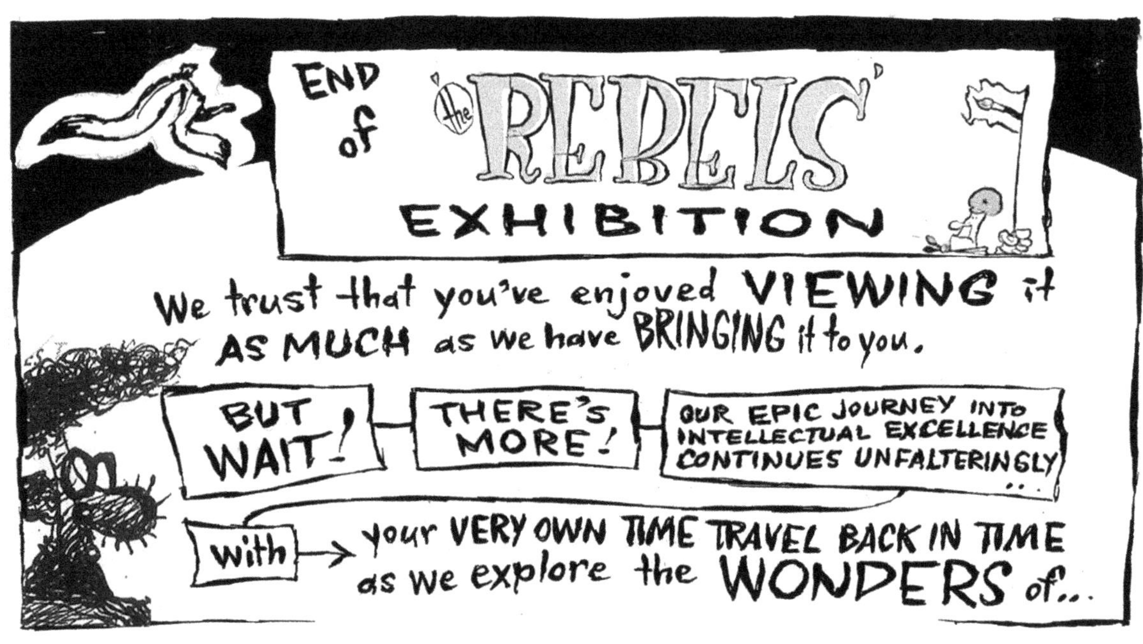

And where better to start than at the very

CRADLE of CIVILIZATION

itself... →

So sit back now, won't you, and **BASK** in the **GLOW** of the

of Our Land Girt by Sea!

The Opera House

IN 1957, THE GREAT DANISH ADVENTURER AND ARCHITECT, **JØRN UTZON**, SET OFF ON A PERILOUS OCEAN **VOYAGE TO AUSTRALIA.** THE OBJECTIVES OF UTZON'S JOURNEY WERE TWO-FOLD.

(FOLD 1 AND FOLD 2.)

* A ROLLICKING OLD DANISH SEA SHANTY.

FIRSTLY... ...UTZON WOULD RETRACE THE ROUTE TAKEN **CENTURIES** BEFORE BY THE GREAT DANISH EXPLORER AND PILLAGER, STIG LARS DAGGERSKØBSKERDØESKER WHO DISCOVERED AUSTRALIA IN 1375 A.D. BUT FRANKLY DIDN'T WANT IT.

Fränklysk, Idøn't wänt itsk.

Your loss, our gain, Stig.

SECONDLY... ...UTZON WOULD ENDEAVOUR TO FIND A SUITABLE **AUSTRALIAN** BRIDE FOR CROWN PRINCE LARS OF DENMARK.

Ed: THE **READER** IS REMINDED THAT, AT THIS TIME, DENMARK WAS FIRMLY IN THE GRIP OF 'THE GREAT-SUITABLE-DANISH-ROYAL-BRIDE-**FAMINE**.'

Ed again: Sadly, the famine continues to this day.

UNFORTUNATELY FOR UTZON, AND **ESPECIALLY** FOR CROWN PRINCE LARS, NO SUITABLE AUSTRALIAN BRIDE WAS FOUND FOR CROWN PRINCE LARS.

HOWEVER, THE DESIRED OUTCOME WOULD EVENTUALLY BE ACHIEVED SOME **FOUR** DECADES LATER.

UTZON NOW TURNED HIS ATTENTION TO HIS ARCHITECTURAL ASPIRATIONS.

HE SUBMITTED A RADICAL PLAN TO DESIGN A **COMPLETELY NEW CITY THAT WOULD BE BUILT FROM SCRATCH, ON SHEEP PADDOCKS** LOCATED HALFWAY BETWEEN TWO EXISTING MAJOR CITIES.

ESSENTIAL TO UTZEN'S **NEW CITY** CONCEPT WAS A ROAD SYSTEM DESIGN INCORPORATING A NETWORK OF FENG-SHUI-FRIENDLY, RADIATING INTERCONNECTING CIRCLES.

NATURALLY, THE PLAN WAS **PANNED** BY GOVERNMENT AND MEDIA ALIKE, AS BEING **RIDICULOUS, ILL-CONCEIVED, LAUGHABLE,** AND **TOTALLY INSANE!**

(Besides, it had already been done.)

SIX MONTHS LATER UTZON HAD FULLY RECOVERED, AND WAS RELEASED FROM THE WALTER BURLEY-GRIFFIN MEMORIAL INSTITUTION FOR THE CARE OF DELUSIONAL TOWN PLANNERS AND ARCHITECTS.

IT WAS THEN THAT UTZON RECEIVED HIS BIG BREAK -- A COMMISSION TO DESIGN A CEMENT-AND-GLASS-WALLED MEETING ROOM ON SYDNEY HARBOUR.

IT WAS TO BE CALLED 'THE **UTZON ROOM**.'

INSPIRED BY THE SHAPE OF A SHOE BOX ON HIS STUDIO FLOOR, UTZON USED A GROUND-BREAKING 'RECTANGULAR PRISM' DESIGN FOR THE UTZON ROOM.

THE UTZON ROOM WAS COMPLETED IN THE RECORD-BREAKING TIME OF 3 DAYS, AND UTZON MANAGED TO DO IT WITH A JAW-DROPPING, SHOCK, 'END-OF-PROJECT' BUDGET SURPLUS OF MILLIONS OF DOLLARS!

OVERNIGHT, JØRN UTZON BECAME A NATIONAL HERO, AND WAS HAILED AS 'GLORIOUS ARCHITECTURAL SUPER-STAR LEGEND AND BELOVED DANISH SON OF AUSTRALIA.'

'Jørn' became the most popular Australian BABY BOY'S name from the following year up to the present day.

THEN, USING THE PROJECT'S BUDGET SURPLUS FUNDS, UTZON DESIGNED AND BUILT AN EXTENSION TO THE UTZON ROOM.

To the delight of the Australian public, work was completed after only 2 weeks!

THE 'EXTENSION' WAS SUBSEQUENTLY NAMED 'THE SYDNEY OPERA HOUSE', AFTER THE GREAT AUSTRALIAN TENOR, SIR SIDNEY OPERA-HOUSE. (1867-1923)

AND SO, having thus MASTERED this GEM of Australian History we now EXPAND our HORIZONS and turn our attention to...

THE COMPLETE
HISTORY OF THE WORLD
(ON ONE PAGE!)
NEWS

The DAWN of GRAFFITI

Trojan War Cost-cutting: Peewee of Troy waits inside the Trojan Rabbit.
OW! OW! CRAMP!!!

FASHION FIRSTS
Gladiator Sandals
Ooo, I like the sandals... What do you call them?

HA! HA! HA! Oh, alright, I'll come clean! Ha! Ha! I was just temporarily pulling your COLLECTIVE LEG! . An example of classic ACADEMIC HUMOUR there. You CAN'T cover the ENTIRE HISTORY OF THE WORLD in just ONE PAGE. You need AT LEAST FOUR MORE PAGES to cover THE ENTIRE HISTORY OF THE WORLD,

and more SPECIFICALLY,

AS YOU WELL KNOW, THE MONGOLS WERE SHAVED BALD UNDER GHENGIS KHAN'S DRASTIC RESPONSE TO THE GREAT MONGOLIAN DANDRUFF EPIDEMIC OF 1209. HOWEVER, THE BITTERLY COLD SOUTHERLIES THAT SWEPT ACROSS THE MONGOLIAN STEPPES AND THE GOOSE-BUMPED MONGOLIAN HEAD TOPS, DROVE THE MONGOLIANS TO SEARCH FOR A FUNCTIONAL AND SUITABLY COZY HAIRPIECE SOLUTION.

THEY TURNED TO THE PLUCKY MONGOLIAN FERRET HERDERS WHO WITHIN WEEKS HAD TRAINED THEIR FLOCKS TO MOUNT AND LIE PROSTRATE UPON THE SMOOTH AND EXPECTANT HEADS, IN AN ACT OF FERRET DEVOTION CELEBRATED IN MONGOLIAN FOLKLORE TO THIS DAY.

YURGG YAKKMAN, MODERN DAY MONGOLIAN HISTORIAN, MINSTREL, AND FERRET HERDER.

...and they leapt upon those shiny domes, with a HEY NONNY NO!..

ED. OUR SPECIAL THANKS TO THE MONGOLIAN ARTS COUNCIL AND TOURISM AUTHORITY FOR THEIR GENEROUS GRANT OF 20 YURKKELS FOR EVERY MENTION OF 'MONGOLIAN' IN THIS GROUNDBREAKING HISTORICAL GEM. MONGOLIAN. MONGOLIAN. MONGOLIAN. MONGOLIAN. MONGOLIAN.

LOUIS IMMEDIATELY ORDERED THE MAKING OF A LARGE POWDERY WIG TO COVER HIS UNFORTUNATE 21ST CENTURY STYLE HAIRCUT MALFUNCTION.

IN TIME THE LOUIS XIII WIG ENSEMBLE HAIRSTYLE CAUGHT ON, AND BECAME IMMENSELY POPULAR WITH THE ARISTOCRACY UPON PAIN OF DEATH.

BUT OMINOUS STORM CLOUDS WERE GATHERING ON THE LOUIS XIII WIG HORIZON. (Ed. We researched it. There actually IS a LOUIS XIII WIG HORIZON) PUBLIC SENTIMENT WAS EVENTUALLY TO TURN AGAINST THE WIG, AND ULTIMATELY HARSH (AND SOME WOULD SAY EXCESSIVE) MEASURES WERE EMPLOYED TO BRING ABOUT THE LOUIS XIII WIGS' UNTIMELY END.

WELL, if there's ONE THING we've learned from all this, it's that you CAN'T have HISTORY without...

PEOPLE

ONLY AN ADULT ON BOARD BUT I'M STILL HOPING THAT YOU WON'T CRASH INTO ME

Well, as with every year, it's been very difficult to choose a winner...
10th ANNUAL CONFORMIST AWARDS

APPY RTH DAY
Professor Leebnitz gives Elouise the gift that keeps on giving.

Leonard had never been in a Love Triangle before, and he wasn't sure he liked it...

And while we're on the subject of 'PEOPLE,' here's a word from World-Renowned 'People' Expert and Registered Para-Seamstress, Dr. Talula-May O'Shay...

If there's ONE THING we know about PEOPLE it's that a SIGNIFICANT number of people wear CLOTHES, as International studies have consistently verified. Yet, sadly, we can't address the subject of CLOTHING without being COMPELLED to CONFRONT the scandalously UGLY REALITY of the SEEDY UNDERBELLY of the GARMENT TRADE.

I refer here, of course, to... →

WARNING Read **ONLY** you who **DARE**.!

Our investigative GARMENT REPORTER Sven O'Flaherty has THIS report..

Forget WATERGATE!

Forget the MRS. O'GOMEZ THE SCHOOL CANTEEN LADY'S BRIBERY-FOR-EXTRA TIM-TAMS SCANDAL!...

WE NOW BRING YOU...

The CUTTING EDGE Investigative Cartoon-o-Journalistic COUP that BLOWS THE LID on...

The GREAT 'Let's-Get-THE CONSUMERS-to-Pay-US-to-Advertise-OUR-BIG BRAND LABEL CLOTHING [FOR FREE]! on the Very Items of Clothing THEY Buy From US' SCAM

IT BEGAN IN AN 82nd FLOOR OFFICE OF A 'BIG-BRAND' CLOTHING CORPORATION...

* No, I don't know what this means either

A 'THINK TANK' BETWEEN THE 'MANAGEMENT' AND THE 'CREATIVES'

THEN, overnight and yet almost imperceptibly, it began...

SOON they became EMBOLDENED to go where NO BIG BRAND NAME ADVERTISING had GONE BEFORE...

DISTURBING IMAGERY INDEED!

But that was not the END of the PERFIDY! That was merely the GATHERING of the MOMENTUM of the PERFIDY.

The next step was as SWIFT as it was CUNNING.

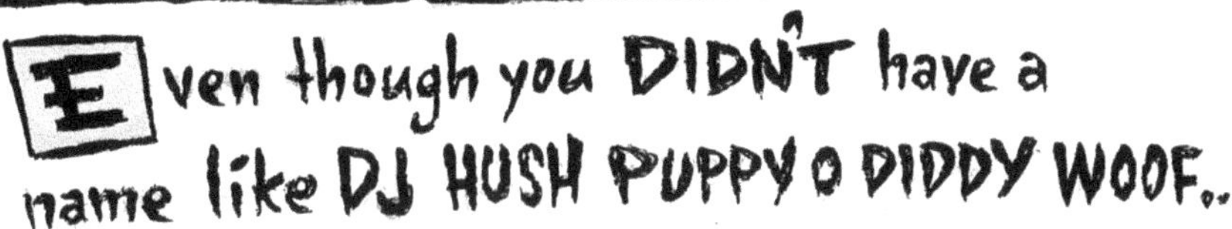

Even though you DIDN'T have a name like DJ HUSH PUPPY O DIDDY WOOF...

...and even though you didn't have any BLING...

...or live in a CRIB...

(No, I don't get this one either)

or have any STREET CRED...

...or have your automobile PIMPED...

...you were informed by the POPULAR CULTURE WING of the BIG BRAND NAME CLOTHING LABELS that you had a...

BOOTY*

* Or apparently if you possessed a particularly FINE one, you had a BOO-TAY

No sooner were you made aware that you had a 'BOOTY', then the BIG BRAND NAME CLOTHING MANUFACTURERS began to...

.. ADVERTISE ON IT!
GLUTE

That's right, people!!
From RIGHT UNDER YOUR NOSES you'd had your BOOTIES HIJACKED by the BIG BRAND-NAME CLOTHING LABELS.
You were the VICTIMS of BOOTY-JACKING!

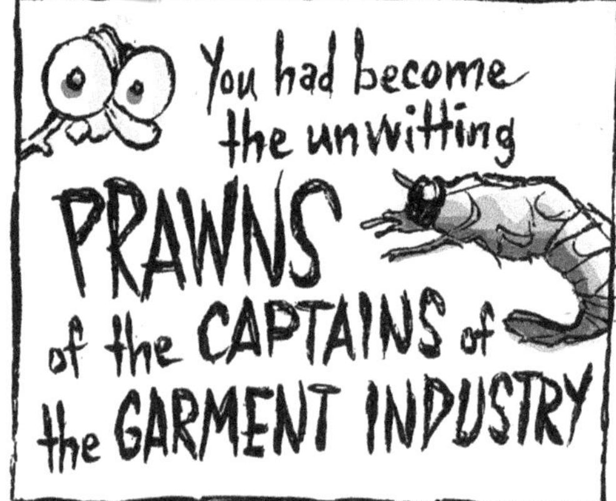
You had become the unwitting PRAWNS of the CAPTAINS of the GARMENT INDUSTRY

To them you were NOTHING but their MINDLESS ADVERTISING SANDWICH BOARDS
FREE AD SPACE AVAILABLE

And they knew NO SHAME!
This SIZE XXXXL will be PERFECT for you! PLUS it will give MAXIMUM BRAND-NAME-RECOGNITION EXPOSURE...
But I take a SIZE 'S'
SALES
BIG T

Here's WHAT, consumers, HERE'S WHAT !!!

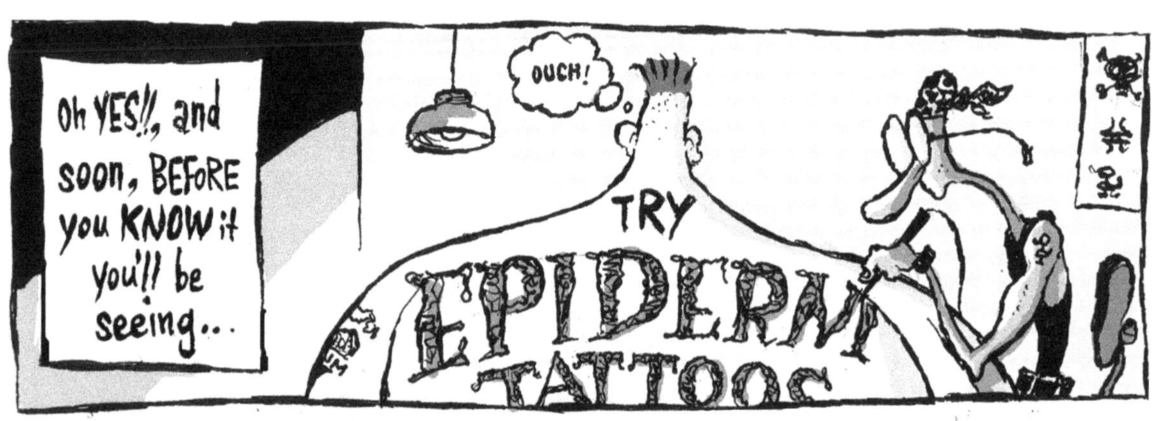
Oh YES!!, and soon, BEFORE you KNOW it you'll be seeing...
OUCH!
TRY
EPIDERM
TATTOOS

Then THIS...
WEAR SHULTZ™ HOSPITAL GOWNS
And THIS!!
DAISY PUSHER™
The COFFIN YOU CAN TRUST
That's IT!!!
ENOUGH is ENOUGH, I say!!
SLAM!!
Something MUST be done about it NOW!!... It's time to...
...OCCUPY YOUR CLOTHES!!

AND HERE ARE SOME NIFTY IDEAS ON JUST HOW YOU CAN RECLAIM YOUR APPAREL

1 Get your existing CLOTHING CORPORATION FREE-ADVERTISING CLOTHES and simply CUT OUT the OFFENDING BRAND NAME.

2 Why not SEW your OWN Rustic-Charm, Retro NON-BRAND-NAME ADVERTISING Shirts, Tights and Undies?!

3 But WHY stop THERE?!!

BUY one of our SPECIAL 'APPROPRIATE MESSAGE' T-SHIRTS and do YOUR PART to STEM THE TIDE of MINDLESS CONSUMERISM.

SUBSCRIBE to 'SAY NO TO MINDLESS CONSUMERISM' Magazine TODAY!

Buy ONE, get ONE FREE! HURRY while STOCKS LAST!!

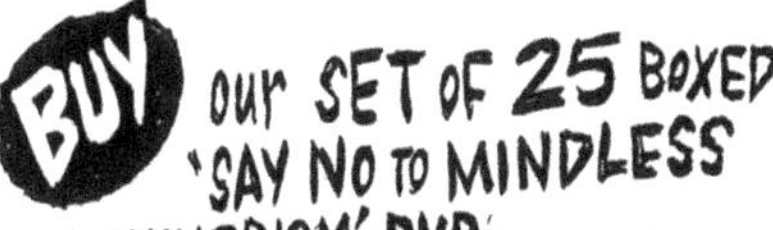

BUY our SET OF 25 BOXED 'SAY NO TO MINDLESS CONSUMERISM' DVD's & YOU WILL RECEIVE A 'SAY NO to etc. etc.' COFFEE MUG ABSOLUTELY FREE!

EVERYTHING MUST GO!!!

BONUS Fashion Tips for the Gentleman About Town

1 Hats

The DO and DON'T of HOW TO WEAR YOUR HAT

INCORRECT

Hmm... Unfortunately this hat is being worn in a DULL and UNIMAGINATIVE manner.

CORRECT

Ah, now THAT's better! Notice the ANGLE as the hat is now being worn at a JAUNTY TILT.

2 Trousers!

Versatile and FUN! Here are 2 WINNING WAYS to wear YOUR Trousers

A The GEORGE CLOONEY Trouser METHOD

NOTE that the WAIST-LINE of the TROUSERS is in perfect ALIGNMENT with the WAIST-LINE of the MODEL.

B The JOHNNY DEPP Trouser METHOD

Here the WAIST-LINE of the TROUSERS is completely FLUSH with the area just BELOW the ARMPITS.

NOTE the ATTRACTIVE and WELL-VENTILATED area where the SHINS and WHITE SOCKS are in full view of ADMIRING VIEWERS

Which brings us almost effortlessly to leading **PHILOSOPHER** and **TROUSERS MODEL**, Dr. Hans Kneesantoes, with his profound yet refreshingly **TEMERARIOUS** take on 'The **HUMAN CONDITION**'..

We are **BIRDS** of a **FEATHER**

We are **ALL** in the **SAME BOAT**

Indeed, you could **VERY WELL SAY**..

We are all **COWS** in the same **CAR**

So then indeedy, how much ought we all to jolly well...

AND ON THAT CHEERY NOTE...

Uh... 'LADIES and GENTLEMEN' Readers. It is with not inconsiderable pleasure that I... that my associate and I...

PROUDLY present...

COWS in CARS!

STUNT-RIDIN' DAIRY-DEVILS!
Maurice and Dimitri, the 2 Founding Members of 'MAD COW MOTOR STUNT TEAM' pull off their trademark, Adrenalin-pumping, '2 WHEEL 1 HOOF HANDSTAND' on their Classic 1962 Turbo-charged V8 Hillman Hercules (Manual 4 door)

Sergeant Harry Hereford of the Highway Bovine Squad in a high speed chase after some cow hoon juvenile offender motoring enthusiasts.

Frankie and Delores enjoying popcorn and soda pop as they watch their favourite movie ('Grease - the Cow Years') at the Drive-In.

Jermaine Jersey (cow slash mechanic) in an uncharacteristic moment of absent-mindedness as he operates the hydraulic car hoist.

Chuck and Chico, young cow hoon offender motoring enthusiasts in their 1969 Vauxhall Vigilante Mark II with their hoofs to the floor, BURNING RUBBER at a cool 60 kph

Thrilling COW MONSTER TRUCK action as ANTON ANGUS powers his way into the BOVINE MONSTER TRUCK HALL of FAME with this EPIC POWER JUMP at the WORLD CHAMPIONSHIPS in UDDERVILLE, ALABAMA

Epilogue to *Cows in Cars*

AND SO we reach our destination, our SURPRISING end to 'CARTOONS, COMICS, and COWS in CARS'

I say 'SURPRISING' in the sense that you may NOT have expected, as you began this CARTOON-and-COMIC-READING-ADVENTURE on Page 1, that your JOURNEY would end with you looking at a picture of a COW named ANTON driving a MONSTER TRUCK.

Yet this is only conjecture on my part. That may have been PRECISELY what you expected to see. You CAN, after all, be UNPREDICTABLE in that way as you have proved time and time again!

I can only trust that YOU'VE enjoyed reading this book as much as I'VE enjoyed eating LEMON MERINGUE pie, taking LONG WALKS on the BEACH, and watching CLASSIC 50's Black-and-White MOVIES in my PYJAMAS.

Afterlogue to the Epilogue

Above: The cartoonist in a PHOTO-SHOOT, both COMPOSITIONALLY STUNNING and BREATH-TAKING in its ORIGINALITY, crosses Abbey Road with John, Paul, Stig, and Bubbles, members of legendary 'Brit-Pop' band, 'The Tiny Beatles.'

THE END

or is it... perhaps...
THE BEGINNING?

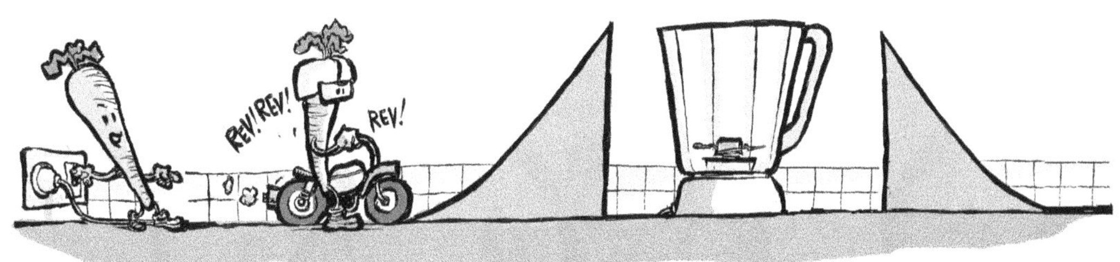

No, I'm pretty sure this **IS THE END**

Yes, this is **ABSOLUTELY** the last **ACTUAL** page.

OF THIS book.

Well, I was wrong about that LAST PAGE being the last page.
I'm fairly sure now that this one really IS the LAST PAGE.

COMICOZ is a registered Australian business (ABN 80 784 984 690) which aims to recognise comics' contribution to and depiction of our Australian culture. It is committed to preserving a permanent collection of Australian comics and cartoon strips.

Nat Karmichael, principal behind COMICOZ, welcomes feedback about 'Rob Feldman's CARTOONS, COMICS, and COWS in CARS.' You can contact Nat by any of the following means...

email: comicoz@live.com.au
web: www.comicoz.com
mail: Comicoz
P.O. BOX 187
MARGATE BEACH, 4019
Queensland (Australia)

Okay, THIS is the last page for SURE.

I just checked.